WORLD WAR II IN EUROPE

"America Goes to War"

R. Conrad Stein

—American War Series—

ENSLOW PUBLISHERS, INC.

Bloy St. & Ramsey Ave.   P.O. Box 38
Box 777   Aldershot
Hillside, N.J. 07205   Hants GU12 6BP
U.S.A   U.K.

Library of Congress Cataloging-in-Publication Data

Stein, R. Conrad.
    World War II in Europe : "America goes to war" / R. Conrad Stein.
      p. cm. — (American war series)
    Includes bibliographical references and index.
    ISBN 0-89490-525-2
    1. World War, 1939-1945—Campaigns—Western—Juvenile
literature. 2. World War, 1939-1945—Campaigns—Eastern—Juvenile
literature. 3. World War, 1939-1945—United States—Juvenile
literature. [1. World War, 1939-1945—Campaigns—Europe.] I. Title.
II. Title: World War Two in Europe. III. Title: World War 2 in
Europe. IV. Series.
D756.3.S74 1994
940.54'0973—dc20   93-47396
                                         CIP
                                         AC
Printed in the United States of America

10 9 8 7 6 5 4 3 2 1

Illustration Credits:
Courtesy of the Aberdeen Proving Grounds Museum, p. 30; Prints and
Photographs Division, Library of Congress, p. 44, Earl McElfresh,
McElfresh Map Company, pp. 27, 79, 114; National Air and Space
Museum, Smithsonian Institution, pp. 71, 93 ; National Archives, pp. 7,
11, 13, 15, 19, 20, 22, 23, 25, 28, 35, 37, 38, 41, 48, 51, 56, 60, 63, 65,
69, 72, 77, 80, 82, 83, 91, 95, 97, 101, 105, 109, 111, 113.

Cover Illustration:
Courtesy of the U.S. Army Art Activity.

Contents

Foreword

In 1984 the Chicago writer Studs Terkel compiled a book called *The Good War*. The book was a collection of interviews—memories of what people did during World War II. It was called *The "Good" War*, because it seemed to most Americans at the time to be a conflict pitting good against evil. There was truth to that somewhat one-sided American belief. Practically everyone today agrees Nazi Germany and Imperial Japan were wicked empires and the world is a far better place without them. But to call a war good even if it eradicated an evil is to ignore the nature of the war. As Studs Terkel said, "the adjective 'good' mated to the noun 'war' is incongruous."

The European War was especially cruel because it was waged on a crowded continent. Women, children, and elderly people were killed by the millions. Campaigns in Italy, Germany, France, and Russia destroyed families, shattered minds, and erased the work of ancient cultures. Those who fought in Europe found little good in the war. An American who endured many months of hellish European fighting told Terkel, "No war can be just. During combat, I would say to myself, this whole damn thing isn't worth one drop of American blood, or anyone's blood."

Still, the European War was an indelible chapter in world history, one that saw the victorious Allied armies crushing a powerful nation led by a madman. But the vast majority of men and women who suffered through the war agree, it is one episode in history that should never repeat itself.

The victor [in this war] will never be asked if he told the truth.
　　　—Adolf Hitler

1 Canned Goods

Early morning, August 31, 1939. No doubt the thirteen German convicts were confused when they were ordered out of a prison camp and driven to a schoolhouse in eastern Germany near the Polish border. The men had been sentenced to death for various crimes, and they grimly awaited their fate in jail. Now they surely wondered why they were being brought to a school building. Inside a classroom, German officers ordered the men to undress and put on Polish army uniforms. A doctor then gave twelve of the thirteen prisoners injections of a poisonous drug. No one knows if the criminals fought the officers, or if they meekly accepted their deaths.

Guards dragged the corpses to a wooded area, where

they were sprayed with machine-gun fire. Pictures were taken, and journalists were called to the scene. The journalists were told the bodies were those of Polish invaders who had been gunned down while attacking Germany.

Next the officers drove the remaining prisoner to the nearby German town of Gleiwitz. Now dressed in civilian clothes, the officers broke into the town's radio station. One of the officers spoke fluent Polish. Over the radio he gave an impassioned speech announcing the shocking news that Poland had just invaded Germany. At the conclusion of the speech, the remaining convict was shot several times in the chest and was left facedown on the floor. A German spokesman later stated the convict was a firebrand Pole who seized the radio station, delivered an angry declaration of war, and was then killed by German patriots.

The bizarre and cruel events at the Polish border were part of a top secret German plan called Operation Canned Goods. The "canned goods" were the hapless convicts. They were used as stage props in a deceptive drama designed to justify a German invasion of Poland.

At 10 A.M. the next morning, the German leader, Adolf Hitler, spoke over the radio: "Last night Polish soldiers fired on our territory. . . . From now on, bombs will be met with bombs." At the very moment Hitler made his speech, the German army, which had been massed at the frontier for weeks, was sweeping into Poland.

Germans were stunned by the news. Surely this meant war, not only with Poland, but also with her powerful allies, Great Britain and France. The American

German troops sweep through Warsaw, Poland in September, 1939.

newspaper writer William Shirer, who was stationed in Berlin, noted in his diary, "Everybody against the war. People talking openly. How can a country go into a major war with the people dead set against it?"[1]

Some Germans believed France and Great Britain would do nothing in defense of Poland because European nations seemed to be afraid of Adolf Hitler. In March of 1936 German troops occupied the Rhineland, a district on the border with France, which, according to The Treaty of Versailles, was off-limits to the German army. A year later Hitler sent his armies into Austria and made that nation a part of greater Germany. Finally, in late September 1938, Germany seized the Sudetenland, a region of Czechoslovakia. In each of these bloodless conquests, France and Great Britain threatened to wage war but stopped short of using military force to halt Germany's aggressions.

Poland, however, was final proof that appeasing Hitler simply fueled his greed for greater territorial gains. Three days after the invasion of Poland, both Britain and France declared war on Germany. World War II in Europe had begun. German leaders were shocked and dismayed at the French and British stand. Hermann Goering, chief of the German air force and number two man in the government, said to his aide, "If we lose this war, then God help us."

We shall fight on the beaches,
we shall fight on the landing grounds,
we shall fight on the fields and in the streets;
we will never surrender.
    —Winston Churchill

2 The Swastika Spreads Across Europe

 World War I bled Europe. When the war ended in 1918, France had lost 1.4 million soldiers, Britain counted 900,000 dead, Italy 650,000, and Russia had so many men and women killed it was impossible to count them. Germany was the major defeated power; it had lost 1.8 million troops. The Allied countries, led by Britain and France, imposed a harsh peace on Germany. Many historians believe the Versailles Treaty, the final pact that ended World War I, was a blueprint to begin World War II. According to terms of the Versailles Treaty, Germany lost vital territory. The Allies demanded $33 billion in repayment for war damages. The treaty forbade Germany from ever again fielding a large army.

The Rise of the Nazis

The German postwar government tried to pay its war debts by printing more money. The printing effort resulted in disastrous inflation. A loaf of bread that once cost 1 mark zoomed to 1 million marks. Berliners told a grim story about a woman who went shopping carrying a basket full of mark notes. She put the basket down for a minute and returned to find the marks scattered on the sidewalk but her basket stolen. The inflation shattered the German economy. Jobless men, many of whom were war veterans, roamed the streets, hungry and desperate. Dozens of political parties sprang up, each promising the German people they would end the economic chaos. One of those political organizations was the Nazi Party headed by Adolf Hitler.

Hitler was born April 20, 1889, at the Austrian town of Braunau, which was near the German border. As a youth he dreamed about becoming an artist, but he lacked the patience to labor long hours over a canvas. At sixteen he dropped out of school and drifted to Vienna, the Austrian capital, where he performed odd jobs including carrying suitcases at the railroad station. He enlisted in the German army during World War I and won two medals for bravery. Once he was wounded in the leg and another time he was temporarily blinded during a gas attack. In 1919 he joined the infant Nazi Party and quickly rose to be its chief.

The future dictator of Germany was a fiery speaker who pounded his fists and shouted wildly to drive home a point. He promised a new government that would

Adolf Hitler at a Nazi rally in the city of Nuremberg, Germany, 1928.

control runaway prices, give the people work, and erase the memory of World War I defeat. In his speeches he often alluded to pet racial theories. He told the Germans they were the master race, superior to all others. The Slavic people to the east of Germany were the *untermenschen*, a lower order of human beings. He reserved a special hatred for Jews. He once said, "Was there any shady undertaking, any form of foulness . . . in which one Jew did not take part?"

In a 1932 national election, the Nazi Party won 40 percent of the German vote. This strong showing forced President Paul von Hindenburg to appoint Hitler chancellor (prime minister) of Germany. Hindenburg died in 1934, and Hitler took complete command of the nation. Throughout Germany he was now called *Der Fuhrer*, "the leader."

Hitler and the Nazis imposed a new order on Germany. All aspects of national life—especially the schools—were controlled by the state. New textbooks appeared, portraying war as a field of honor where boys rose to become heroes. All boys and girls were required to join the Hitler Youth, a military version of the Boy Scouts or Girl Scouts. One of the Hitler Youth slogans, which they recited in unison during meetings, said, "Your name, my Fuhrer, is the happiness of youth; your name, my Fuhrer, is for us everlasting life."

Like the emperors of ancient Rome, the Nazis gave the people "bread and circuses." Bread came in the form of an improved economy and an end to the crippling inflation. Circuses were presented as part of a massive

The Luftwaffe auxillary of the Hitler Youth study aeronautics.

effort to bury the sting of defeat in the First World War. Great pageants featuring thousands of gymnasts were held in sports stadiums. Parades accompanied by brass bands wound through city streets. Above all these events waved the banner of the twisted cross, the swastika. Before it became the symbol of the Nazi Party, the swastika was drawn by ancient people and it meant, ironically, good luck.

Slowly and deliberately, Hitler's government prepared the nation for war. The Fuhrer ignored the Versailles Treaty and rearmed Germany. He and the country's military leaders foresaw a new era of fast-moving warfare and insisted the German army be equipped with tanks, trucks, and airplanes. Hitler said the German people needed *lebensraum,* "living room," in eastern Europe. Britain and France were to be taught a military lesson they would never forget, but Germany's ultimate destiny was to carve out a new empire to the east in the land of the inferior Slavs. Seeking *lebensraum,* Hitler's army invaded Poland and started the European chapter of World War II.

Blitzkrieg

In Poland, Hitler's army electrified the world. Most European generals believed this war would be a repeat of the previous one, an ordeal of trench fighting where victory was measured in a few hundred yards of muddy ground. But now the Germans raced over Poland on tank treads and on rubber wheels. Never before had military men seen armies move with such breathtaking

Adolf Hitler triumphantly returns to Vienna, Austria, 1939.

speed. The Germans called this war of swift deployment *blitzkrieg* or "lightning war." Roaring above the German armies was a fleet of modern aircraft. Gull-winged black dive bombers, called Stukas, screamed out of the sky to dump five-hundred pound bombs on Polish defenders. Some of the Stukas had sirens attached to their wings to make them sound even more fearsome in a dive.

The Poles fought valiantly, but their army was hopelessly outclassed. The country fell after less than four weeks of fighting. On September 17, 1939, Russia attacked Poland from the east. The Russian attack was part of a secret deal cooked up between Hitler and the Soviet dictator, Joseph Stalin. When the fighting ceased, Russia and Germany divided their defeated neighbor.

In the west, along Germany's border with France, an uneasy quiet prevailed. British newspapers called the situation on the French border a "Phony War," while the Germans joked it was "Sitzkrieg," (Sitting-Down War). Taking advantage of the Western Allies' inaction, Germany invaded Denmark and Norway on April 9, 1940. In Norway, the Germans unveiled the latest in their bag of tricks by capturing airfields with paratroopers. After overwhelming surprised defenders on the airfields, the paratroopers held the fields until cargo planes carrying infantry could land. Norway was forced to surrender after a month of fighting, and the Germans acquired excellent bases for their submarines to use in the North Sea.

A new chapter of blitzkrieg exploded on May 10, 1940, when Hitler sent his armored divisions into the neutral countries of Belgium, Luxembourg, and the

Netherlands. Between the wars French engineers had built, along their border with Germany, a 250-mile long series of fortresses called the Maginot Line. Gun emplacements on the line were protected by concrete walls, many of which were ten feet thick. Rather than attack the Maginot Line directly, German generals went around it by driving into the neutral countries and through a thickly wooded area called the Ardennes Forest. Traveling with the lead tanks in the Ardennes were units of combat engineers called *Sturmpionieren*. Using dynamite and bulldozers, the engineers created roads in rugged forest land where not even a path existed before. North of the forest, specially trained German combat teams conquered forts built by the Belgium army.

The German dash around the Maginot Line had the effect of uncorking a bottle. Thousands of German troops poured into France. Their lightning war tactics stunned enemy generals. The French army, which had fought valiantly in World War I, reeled backward in a panicked retreat. Each time the French tried to make a stand, they were pounded by German artillery and by bombs falling from screaming Stukas. A French officer wrote, "Our gunners stopped firing and went to the ground. The infantry cowered in their trenches, dazed by the crash of bombs and the shriek of dive bombers."

In the north a huge force of French, British, and Belgian troops found itself surrounded near the port city of Dunkirk. The British organized a makeshift fleet composed of fishing boats and pleasure craft to rescue the trapped men. The ships inched up to shore while desperate soldiers waded or swam to them. The entire operation took place under a hail of German artillery fire and almost constant air attacks. Amazingly the British evacuated some 340,000 men over nine days. Newspapers in Britain hailed the mass rescue as the "Miracle of Dunkirk." But most British citizens, including the newly sworn-in prime minister, Winston Churchill, knew that wars were not won by evacuations.

On June 10, 1940, when the French were near defeat, Italian Premier Benito Mussolini declared war on France. Mussolini and Hitler were allies, and the Italian leader now wanted to join in the spoils of victory. Across the ocean, American President Franklin Delano Roosevelt said of Mussolini's move, "The hand that held the dagger has struck it into the back of its neighbor."

The German army entered Paris on June 14, 1940. Soon afterward, France surrendered. On June 18th, Winston Churchill addressed Great Britain by radio: "The battle of France is over. I expect the Battle of Britain is about to begin . . . Let us therefore brace ourselves to our duties, and so bear ourselves that, if the British Empire and its commonwealth last for a thousand years, men will say, 'This was their finest hour.' "[1]

Britain Stands Alone

"This is London, ten minutes before five in the morning. Tonight's raid has been widespread. London is again the main target . . . The outskirts appear to have suffered the hardest pounding."[2] With these words, spoken on October 10, 1940, the American radio reporter Edward R. Murrow

A Frenchman weeps as the triumphant German army marches through Paris on June 14, 1940.

Air raid officials scan the sky above London for German bombers during "The Blitz." St. Paul's Cathedral stands in the background.

began his nightly broadcast to listeners in the United States. Night after night Murrow reported terrible bombing raids while standing on the roof of a London office building. To American listeners he described the hell around him—searchlights piercing the night, sirens howling, antiaircraft fire thundering, dozens of fires burning, and bombs screaming out of the sky.

During 1940 and early 1941 Britain fought Germany alone in the skies above England and in the waters of the Atlantic. For civilians, the air war was the most devastating. Londoners called it "The Blitz."

The air war began with the German air force, the Luftwaffe, bombing airfields used by the Royal Air Force, the RAF. The object of the German attacks was to destroy the RAF so the German navy and army could invade British shores. British pilots flew the Spitfire, a highly maneuverable fighter aircraft which could reach a speed of 370 mph. The Germans' prime fighter was the Messerschmitt—20 mph slower than the Spitfire, but able to climb higher.

The Messerschmitt suffered a disadvantage in what was called the Battle of Britain because it took off from fields in France and had only enough fuel for ten or fifteen minutes of combat in English skies. Because of the fuel limitations, German bombers often had to attack British airfields unescorted by fighters. The Luftwaffe lost two planes for every RAF plane it destroyed. The losses caused the Germans to shift their tactics from attacking airfields during the day to bombing cities during the night. The agony of the Blitz began.

Throughout the fall and winter of 1940-41 British men, women, and children heard the fearful whine of aircraft sirens and scrambled for their shelters. The London Underground, the city's subway system, served as a major shelter for civilians. Thousands of people slept in the Underground each night. When bombs rained down, they prayed, and family members clutched each other tightly, wincing with each deadly thud. A direct hit, even on a subway shelter, could bury the people under tons of debris. A young boy named Bernard Kops remembered

Children of London made homeless by German bombers during the Blitz of late 1940.

St. Paul's Cathedral in the center of London standing proud after a terrible German air raid on December 29, 1940.

shivering in a London shelter with his family as bombs shook the earth and plaster tumbled from the ceiling.

> The men started to play cards and the women tried a little sing-song," Kops said. "But every so often the women's fists shook at the ceiling, cursing the explosions, Germany, Hitler. 'May he [Hitler] die from a lingering tumor,' my mother wailed. 'That's too good for him,' Aunt Sarah said. I sat under the table where the men were playing cards, screwing up my eyes and covering my ears, counting the explosions.[3]

While the bombs burst over British cities, a savage submarine war was fought in the Atlantic. Britain suffered from a lack of natural resources, especially oil. Wartime England needed supplies from at least one thousand cargo ships a month in order to survive and fight back. But at sea the slow-moving cargo ships presented fat targets for German U-boats. Often the submarines operated in "wolf packs," groups of five to eight boats. In 1941 alone, wolf packs sank 445 British ships against the loss of only 38 submarines. The U-boat offensive strangled Great Britain. Winston Churchill later wrote, "The only thing that ever really frightened me during the war was the U-boat peril."[4]

Somehow Britain survived the terrible winter of 1940-41. The air raids came almost nightly, but the Luftwaffe failed to destroy the RAF. In the Atlantic the British navy began to find more effective means of fighting the U-boats. By the spring of 1941, a feeling of confidence dawned over Britain. Thousands of city

A convoy of American and British ships off the coast of Iceland.

dwellers shoveled up the debris of bombed-out buildings and dug vegetable gardens in the parks. Children joined the effort, and as they worked, they sang a little song:

> *Whistle while you work*
> *Hitler is a twerp*
> *Goering's barmy*
> *So's his army*
> *Whistle while you work.*[5]

Hitler Strikes Russia

In April of 1941 Germany invaded Greece and Yugoslavia. The campaign in Greece was launched to help the Italian army which had marched into that country five months earlier but was driven backward by staunch Greek defenders. In a matter of days, ruthlessly efficient German armored divisions overran both Greece and Yugoslavia. In Yugoslavia, however, thousands of guerrilla fighters retreated to the mountains and battled their German occupiers for the remainder of the war. With the Balkan region now under German control, Hitler turned east to make his most daring move of the war.

"When [the invasion of Russia] commences, the world will hold its breath," said Hitler to his generals. On June 22, 1941, the invasion began as an army of 3 million men, marching along a 2,000-mile front, slammed into Soviet Russia.

By attacking the sprawling Soviet Union, Hitler opened up a war on two fronts—against Britain to the west and against the Soviet Union to the east. A war on two fronts, the German generals believed, would sap

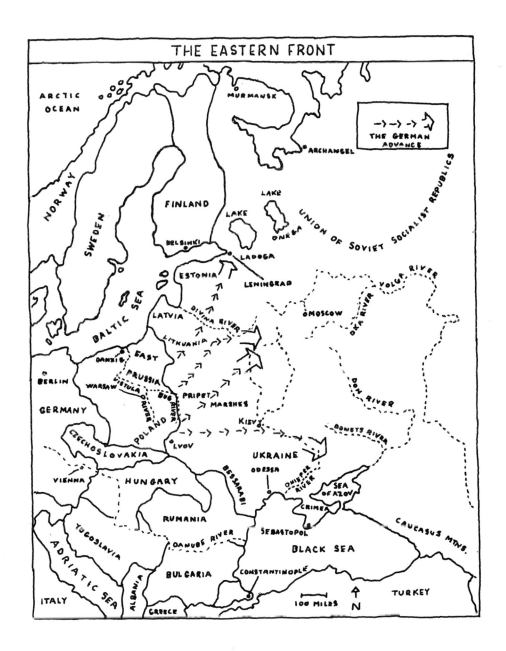

German infantrymen in Russia 1941.

their armies strength and lead to defeat. Heeding the generals' advice, Hitler had made a peace pact with Soviet Premier Joseph Stalin in 1939. The pact allowed Germany to risk war with France, to the west, while enjoying peace with Russia, its powerful neighbor to the east. Now, however, Hitler had thrown his nation into war against Russia at the same time he was fighting the British. Hitler dismissed his generals' worries by arguing that Great Britain was near defeat. Besides, he told the generals, Russia would collapse in a matter of months.

In the opening weeks it appeared Hitler's prediction was correct. Achieving complete surprise, the German Luftwaffe destroyed most of the Russian air force while the planes were still parked on runways. On the ground, the Soviet army was woefully unprepared to repel Germany's sudden attack. One confused army commander radioed his superiors in Moscow, "I am being fired upon. What do I do now?" A general in Moscow accused the man of being drunk.

Over the Russian wheat fields German armored divisions gave a dazzling display of blitzkrieg on its grandest scale. In the first week, German tanks swept 175 miles inside Russia. On June 27 the ancient city of Minsk fell. Along the Baltic coast tanks rolled towards Leningrad. In central Russia two tank columns met at Kiev and closed a trap which encircled six hundred thousand Russian soldiers. By the beginning of October 1941, Russia had lost 2.5 million men and 18,000 tanks.

Despite the devastating losses by the Russians, German soldiers learned to respect the toughness of Russian

Russian T-34 tanks which many German commanders considered to be the best all around armored vehicle of the war.

troops. They fought with dogged tenacity even when surrounded and cut off from supplies. The Germans also encountered, for the first time, a tank that was superior to any of theirs. The Russian T-34 had thick, sloping armor which caused anti-tank shells to bounce harmlessly off its sides. Wide tank treads allowed the T-34 to cross swampy fields where German tanks bogged down. One of Germany's best tank commanders, Heinz Guderian, said, "Numerous Russian T-34's went into action and inflicted heavy losses on the German tanks. Up to this time we had enjoyed tank superiority, but from now on the situation was reversed."[6]

Still the German army pressed eastward. German tanks reached Leningrad in late October, and the city was surrounded and besieged. In the winter of 1941-42, some four thousand Leningraders died each day from starvation. Also in late October German troops moved to within forty miles of Moscow, the Russian capital. Then, in November, a miserable rain fell for days turning Russia's dirt roads into oozing mud which stopped tanks and trucks. Taking advantage of the Germans' struggle with the roads, Russian leaders called on civilians and reserve troops to dig trenches and defend the capital city. The Russians fought with a brand of courage that astounded the Germans. As snow fell and fierce winds howled over central Russia, the Germans at the gates of Moscow were forced to fall back. For the first time in World War II, the seemingly invincible German army tasted defeat.

*We shall not be able to claim that we have
gained total victory in this war if any vestige
[of Nazism] . . . is permitted to survive
anywhere in the world.*
  —President Franklin D. Roosevelt

The Tide Turns

While Britain and Russia fought Hitler, the American people engaged in what journalists called the Great Debate. Americans divided into two camps: the isolationists, who believed the United States should avoid the war altogether; and the interventionists, who wanted to aid Hitler's enemies. The isolationists pointed out that more than one hundred thousand Americans lost their lives in World War I, and the nation gained little as a result. The interventionists argued that a Nazi victory in Europe would plunge mankind into a new dark age.

The Great Debate
The Great Debate intensified when Germany invaded Russia in June of 1941. Russia was the citadel of world

communism, a political system hated by most Americans. Also, the Russian leader, Joseph Stalin, was a dictator, in many ways as ruthless as Hitler himself. Millions of Americans took the attitude that their nation should simply let the two international gangsters fight between themselves and weaken each other in the process.

On December 7, 1941, the Great Debate ended when a radio operator in the naval department at Washington, D.C., received a shocking message: AIR RAID. PEARL HARBOR. THIS IS NO DRILL. In the next twenty-four hours, more numbing news dispatches came to Washington from the naval base at Pearl Harbor in Hawaii. The Japanese had launched a sneak attack, killing more than two thousand Americans. At least eighteen ships, including the battleship *Arizona,* were sunk. The following day a solemn-faced President Roosevelt spoke before Congress. He called December 7, 1941, "a day which will live in infamy." The President asked for and received a declaration of war against Japan.

Three days after Pearl Harbor, Germany and its ally, Italy, declared war on the United States. By going to war with America, Hitler seemed to be needlessly adding to his list of enemies. Germany had a military alliance with Japan, and Hitler claimed he declared war in Japan's support. But most historians conclude Hitler went to war with America for two reasons: first, he believed war with the United States was inevitable anyway; second, he thought it would take the United States at least two years

The U.S.S. *Arizona* was sunk December 7, 1941 during the raid on
Pearl Harbor by the Japanese.

to raise an army and build enough ships to bring that army to Europe.

North Africa

Fighting began in the North African desert in the winter of 1941 when British and Italian armies clashed in Egypt. To aid the Italians, Hitler sent a crack tank corps headed by General Irwin Rommel to North Africa. Over the desert sands Rommel moved his tank units with the skill of a master chess player, always striking the British where they least expected a blow. To the British he became a mystical figure, cursed and respected as "The Desert Fox".

Rommel hoped to capture the Suez Canal, Britain's lifeline to the Arabian oil fields. Through the first half of 1942, the British and the German-led Africa Corps fought a series of seesaw tank battles over waves of desert hills. Thousands of troops on both sides were killed, but neither the British nor the Germans could claim victory.

Finally, in August 1942, Winston Churchill appointed a new general—Bernard Montgomery—to lead the British forces in the desert. Montgomery concentrated his men and tanks on a small front near the Egyptian city of El Alamein. He backed his forces with more than one thousand big guns. On the moonlit night of October 23, 1942, British artillery officers issued a one-word command:

Fire!

The desert floor shook from the force of exploding shells. Rommel was overwhelmed by superior numbers

German General Irwin Rommel in the North African desert in
1941. Rommel was nicknamed "The Desert Fox" by the British.

British General Bernard Montgomery watches his tanks in action in North Africa.

of British guns and tanks. He ordered his famed Africa Corps to retreat, but he was temporarily stopped by an urgent telegram from Adolf Hitler: "Hold fast, never retreat, hurl every gun and every man into the fray." Rommel ignored the stand-till-death order and pulled his troops back so they could live to fight another day. He was one of the few German generals who could defy an order from the Fuhrer and live to command again.

As Rommel withdrew from El Alamein, a new enemy appeared to his rear. In early November 1942, some thirty-five thousand American troops splashed ashore along a two hundred-mile-long landing area that stretched from the Atlantic Coast to the Mediterranean cities of Oran and Algiers. This was America's first offensive effort in the European conflict, and it came—much to Hitler's surprise—just eleven months after the declaration of war. The Americans were commanded by a little-known general named Dwight D. Eisenhower.

American troops landed in French North Africa, which was controlled by the Vichy government, a puppet of Germany. At first the Americans found themselves battling French defenders. But General Eisenhower quickly made peace with the Vichy French forces. In securing the peace, he displayed his talents as a diplomat, a skill Eisenhower needed later in the war when he commanded a vast army made up of units from many diverse countries.

American soldiers were untested in the trials of combat. Eisenhower himself had never heard a shot fired off the rifle range. Many Americans fled in panic the first time a squadron of Stuka dive bombers screamed down on them, spitting bullets and dropping bombs. When they edged closer to German ranks, they faced the 88mm gun, the most feared artillery piece of the war. The German 88 fired a high-velocity shell which, when it approached, sounded strangely like a loud zipper being unzipped. One GI (slang for American soldier) said,

> For the average GI '88 fever' is the worst kind you can get. All we knew was that the 88s had a rate of fire running up to twenty rounds a minute, that it could tear apart a low-flying plane or a tank or a troop concentration. Aimed in your direction, it had all the horror of hell.[1]

In February 1943 Rommel struck the Americans at the Kasserine Pass in Tunisia. "A violent tank battle developed," Rommel wrote, "in which the inexperienced Americans were steadily battered down by my tank men—veterans of hundreds of desert battles—and soon large numbers of [American] tanks were blazing on the battlefield . . ."[2] At Kasserine Pass the United States Army lost at least 160 tanks, and some 2,400 GI's surrendered to the Germans.

Although the Americans lost the battle at Kasserine, they began to learn the harsh lessons of warfare. They learned that camouflage could help save a tank or a truck from marauding Stukas. They discovered land mines knocked out enemy tanks even more easily than did heavy anti-tank guns. The infantryman found his entrenching tool—a simple shovel—could save his life

Stuka bombers terrified troops with their screaming and five-hundred pound bombs.

because it enabled him to dig in and survive a heavy bombardment.

By the spring of 1943, Rommel, the desert fox, was on the run in North Africa. From the east rolled the British army, confident after its success at El Alamein. From the west came the Americans, learning as they advanced.

The battle for a key hill, simply called Hill 609, demonstrated the renewed toughness of the American army. Hill 609 overlooked a valley through which the Americans had to advance in order to continue their offensive. For four days in late April 1943, American soldiers struggled up the hill to take ground only to be driven back by stubborn German defenders. During close fighting, Germans and Americans slashed at each other with bayonets, even with shovels. American Sherman tanks were called in to blast Hill 609 with their 75 mm guns. On May 3, 1943 the Americans took the blood-soaked hill, but only after absorbing terrible losses—two hundred dead, seven hundred captured, sixteen hundred wounded.

Relentlessly the American and British armies pressed forward. In the skies Allied fighter planes shot down the dreaded Stukas, and turned on the retreating Germans to bomb and machine-gun their tanks and trucks. A captured German general broke down and cried in front of Allied officers. "I am a general without a command," the German said. "My tanks have been wiped out."

On May 13 the Africa Corps, composed of 240,000 German and Italian troops, was forced to surrender.

General Rommel escaped to Germany. After the North African victory, Winston Churchill looked ahead and glimpsed at the war's final conclusion, "Now this is not the end. It is not even the beginning of the end. But it is, perhaps, the end of the beginning."[3]

The German Ordeal at Stalingrad

Far from North Africa, a pivotal battle was forming at the Russian city of Stalingrad. Holding half a million people, Stalingrad was Russia's third largest city. Now called Volgograd, it was given its old name in 1925 to honor the Soviet dictator. Stalin considered his namesake city to be the pride of the Soviet Union. To the generals defending it he said, "Take not one step backwards."

In August 1942 the Germans pounded Stalingrad with an incredible air raid. More than six hundred planes were mustered, some of them transport aircraft that were pressed into duty as bombers. The city's brick buildings were blown into a tangle of rubble. At least forty thousand civilians were killed in the two-day aerial bombardment. After the planes did their deadly work, the German 6th Army, led by General Friedrich Paulus, approached Stalingrad's outskirts. Paulus was known as an obedient, dependable commander. If Hitler wanted Stalingrad, Paulus intended to deliver the city to him.

Commanding the Russian defenders was a determined general named Vasily Chuikov. He knew tanks and blitzkrieg tactics would be useless on rubble-strewn streets. So, Chuikov ordered his men to hide in the

Prime Minister Winston Churchill inspects an American-made M-3 tank in July, 1941.

wrecked buildings, allow the Germans to approach, and then attack them with rifles and grenades. "Every German soldier must be made to feel he is living under the muzzle of a Russian gun," Chuikov told his troops.

The fight for the city raged for two months. It was an ugly battle, fought street by street, alley by alley, and ruin by ruin. The Germans called it *Rattenkrieg,* War of Rats. One frustrated German soldier said, "We would spend the whole day clearing a street from one end to the other. But at dawn the Russians would start up again, firing from their old positions. It took us some time to discover their trick; they had knocked holes between buildings, and in the night they would run back like rats in the rafters and set up their machine guns."

By November 1942 the German 6th Army occupied 90 percent of Stalingrad. In Berlin, Adolf Hitler was confident the battle for the city had been won. "I wanted to take the city, and . . . we really have," said the German leader. "There are only a few places left there [that are still in Russian hands]."

Then, on November 19, artillery thundered from fronts both north and south of the 6th Army. The Russians were counterattacking, and they had more tanks and heavy guns than the Germans had ever before seen. Two huge tank spearheads sped over the frozen ground to meet at the Don River behind General Paulus and his men. The Germans at Stalingrad—more than a quarter million men—were trapped.

Paulus wanted to fight his way out of the Soviet ring and radioed Berlin for permission. Hitler sent a terse reply: "Hold at all costs." Paulus could scarcely believe the command. He was surrounded. How could he possibly hold his position at Stalingrad?

Hitler had made an incredible decision. He determined the 6th Army was not a surrounded and desperate body of troops. Instead, in his thinking, the men at Stalingrad were defending a fortress and would fight a menacing action behind Soviet lines. Hitler declared he would supply "Fortress Stalingrad" by air. But swirling snow and powerful winds made an airborne supply operation impossible. Fortress Stalingrad, which existed only in Hitler's fantasies, bled and died in the cruel Russian winter.

A German medical officer at Stalingrad named Heinrich Happe wrote,

> In this unearthly cold the breath froze and icicles hung from nostrils and eyelashes . . . Habit and discipline kept us going; that and the flicker of an instinct to stay alive. And when the soldier's mind had become numb, when his strength, his discipline, and his will had been used up, he sank into the snow . . . He lay where he collapsed until it was too late . . . and the wind blew over him and everything was leveled.[4]

Every seven seconds a German soldier died at Stalingrad. Frostbite, disease, and starvation took more lives than did enemy bullets. And every day the Russians pressed closer. On the morning of January 31, 1943, Berlin received its last radio message from Stalingrad: "The Russians are standing at the door of our bunker.

We are destroying our equipment. This station will no longer transmit."

Stalingrad was a disaster for Nazi Germany. Three hundred thousand German men were killed or captured. Of those captured, only five thousand ever returned home. The remainder died in Soviet prison camps. The German army never recovered from the bitter defeat. Historians consider the Battle of Stalingrad to be the major turning point of the European War.

Sicily and Italy

"The paramount task before us is . . . to strike at the soft underbelly [of Europe]," said Winston Churchill in November of 1942. Churchill harbored a passionate belief that victory could be achieved through an invasion of Germany from the south—an advance beginning on the Mediterranean Sea. American officers, led by Army Chief of Staff George Marshall, favored the more direct approach of landing in France and driving east toward Germany. Churchill's will prevailed, and the Allies prepared to invade Sicily and Italy as a means of reaching Germany's "soft underbelly."

On July 10, 1943, British and American soldiers stormed the beaches on the island of Sicily, located off the toe of the boot-shaped Italian peninsula. The Americans were led by General George S. Patton. Tough, arrogant, and profane, Patton had a simple theory of warfare: always move forward and "go like hell." Patton had an intense hatred of the enemy. He once said of the Germans, "We won't just shoot the sonsabitches, we're

General George S. Patton in North Africa, 1942. Patton said of the Germans, "...we're going to cut out their living guts and use them to grease the treads of our tanks."

going to cut out their living guts and use them to grease the treads of our tanks."

With Patton leading, and sometimes kicking, his men forward, the American forces streaked across Sicily and reached the city of Palermo in just two weeks. By capturing Palermo, Patton cut the island of Sicily in two. He then drove toward Messina, hoping to trap the German defenders who were by now in full retreat. But primitive roads and jagged mountains slowed Patton's advance. The bulk of the German army escaped to Italy. Still, all of Sicily was in Allied hands by mid-August 1943. Italy was now the next logical step in the process of piercing the enemy's soft underbelly.

The Italian people were never enthusiastic about the war. Like the Germans, they had been seduced by a man who promised the nation a return to its past glories. But the Italian dictator, Benito Mussolini, did not enjoy Hitler's iron-fisted control over his country. After the disastrous defeats in North Africa and Sicily, Italians demanded Mussolini step down from power. The country's king, Victor Emmanuel, summoned Mussolini to his court and told him, "At this moment you are the most hated man in Italy." Mussolini was imprisoned, but was later freed by a daring German parachute raid. In 1945 Mussolini was captured and executed by an Italian mob.

The downfall of Mussolini was of little benefit to the Americans and the British. The Germans, sensing the coming of an invasion, rushed troops onto the Italian peninsula. The Italian people, once the partners of the Germans, became their captives.

In early September 1943, the Allies struck Italy at two landing areas. The British, led by Montgomery, crossed the narrow Strait of Messina and stormed ashore near the toe of the Italian boot. The Americans, under the command of General Mark Clark, invaded far to the north at the city of Salerno. Montgomery and the British landed virtually without opposition. Salerno was a different and a very tragic story.

Mountainous central Italy offered few places other than Salerno for the Allies to land a large force. The Germans knew this, and placed heavy guns on the hills overlooking Salerno's beaches. The Allied troops rushed from their landing boats into the horror of screaming shells. The men were unable to advance into the withering fire, yet they could not withdraw because their backs were at the sea. Only the steady pounding of heavy guns from Allied warships saved the landing force from obliteration. The battle for Salerno lasted nine days. It cost the Allies thirty-nine hundred men killed and wounded.

From Salerno the Germans withdrew to the north. They were commanded by Field Marshal Albert Kesselring, who was gifted with a superb eye for terrain. He knew the endless mountains of northern Italy were a paradise for a defending army and a hell for an attacking force. Content to fight a defensive war, Kesselring ordered his men to dig trenches in the mountain ranges north of Naples. He fortified the trench line with concrete gun emplacements and thousands of land mines.

An American GI gives blood plasma to a fellow soldier wounded in Sicily.

The German commander created a defensive front so strong he boasted, "The British and the Americans will break their teeth on it."

Instead of being a gateway to Germany, the Italian peninsula proved to be a gigantic bottleneck which hampered Allied progress. War in Italy degenerated into a frustrating stalemate—a crushing reversal for Churchill's dreams and a graveyard for thousands of Allied troops.

The Home Front

Just before the war broke out, Adolf Hitler traveled through German farmland with one of his chief aides, the architect Albert Speer. "Everywhere the farmers left their implements [to welcome us]," Speer noted. "It was a triumphal procession. As the car rolled along, Hitler leaned back to me and exclaimed, 'Heretofore only one other German has been hailed like this: Martin Luther.' "[1]

The New Germany

Hitler was not idly boasting when he compared his popularity to that of Martin Luther, the sixteenth century German religious leader. The Fuhrer had lifted Germany from the despair of World War I. He brought jobs to the jobless and food to the hungry. He promised to build a new Germany that would be the envy of the world.

But under Hitler's leadership, Germans suffered an erosion of their freedoms. At first the loss of liberty did not seem to be shocking. For example, men and women who belonged to political organizations other than the Nazi Party were questioned by the police. Then, as Hitler grew more powerful, those who continued to oppose Nazi rule started to mysteriously disappear in the night. They were taken to places the average German only whispered about—the concentration camps.

Concentration camps were jails and barbed wire enclosed compounds where authorities placed anyone they deemed to be troublemakers, enemies of the new Germany. Communists were troublemakers, and so were Socialists. The definition of a troublemaker broadened over the years. One woman was taken to a camp because she greeted her neighbor by saying, "Good morning," instead of "Heil Hitler!" Another woman was jailed because she refused to hang a picture of Hitler in her living room.

In the camps people were beaten, humiliated, and fed a starvation diet. One young man from Hamburg, who was dragged off to a camp because he joined the Socialist Party, said his guards amused themselves by making him crouch under the table while they played cards, "and when they wanted to urinate, they did it on me."

Jews were a special target for the Nazis. Hitler brought a violent hatred of Jews with him when he rose to power. He blamed Jewish political intrigue for the nation's World War I defeat. He accused Jewish bankers of engineering the crippling inflation of the 1920s and the economic depression of the 1930s. Germany's propaganda minister, Joseph Goebbels, summed up the Nazi creed when he proclaimed, "The Jews are to blame for everything."

The war threw a cloak of secrecy over Europe, allowing the Nazis to build their infamous compounds in the east: Treblenka, Auschwitz, Berkenau, and others. Here prisoners were put to death, either by firing squads or in gas chambers. In addition to Jews, the Nazis imprisoned and murdered Gypsies, homosexuals, the mentally retarded, and the physically disabled. These people were considered imperfect, and therefore not worthy of living in the New Germany. During the war years, Nazi executioners wrote the dark chapter in world history that is now known as the Holocaust.

Germany harbored many groups which attempted to overthrow the Nazis, but the average citizen dared not question the nation's leaders. In fact, after the war, most Germans claimed they knew nothing of the Holocaust. In truth, however, Germans simply ignored or refused to listen to rumors and whispered words concerning the death camps.

Resistance Movements

"It is terrible outside. Day and night more of those poor miserable people are being dragged off . . . Families are torn apart, the men, women, and children all being

German soldiers arrest Jews in Warsaw, Poland. Many Jews were imprisoned and murdered in Nazi concentration camps.

separated. Children coming home from school find their parents have disappeared. Women return from shopping to find their homes shut up and their families gone."[2] Fifteen-year-old Anne Frank wrote these words in her diary on January 13, 1943. At the time, Anne and her family were hiding from the Nazi police in an Amsterdam attic. After spending two years in seclusion, the family was discovered, and Anne died in 1945 at a Nazi concentration camp. Her crime was being Jewish.

The Nazis imposed a rule of terror over all of occupied Europe. Hitler and his lieutenants believed the captive people could be controlled only if they lived in constant terror. But throughout Europe, the slaves defied their masters. The Jews in the city of Warsaw battled the Germans, even though they had no weapons. Prisoners in the death camps rebelled. Underground armies formed in every German-occupied country.

By 1944 France had an underground force totalling almost half a million men and women. Resistance fighters in France were supplied by secret parachute drops from British airplanes. The French patriot Charles de Gaulle, who had escaped to Great Britain after the fall of France, made rousing speeches on the radio urging all French citizens to cooperate with the resistance. Operating usually at night, members of the French Underground sabotaged railroad tracks, blew up bridges, and burned shipping docks.

The Germans struck back by terrorizing communities they believed were aiding the French resistance. Following a sniper attack near the village of

Oradour-sur-Glane, the German army retaliated by shooting all the village men. Then the Germans placed the women and children in the village church and set it on fire. French people were tortured hideously to extract information about the resistance. A teenage girl named Antonia Hunt was imprisoned as a French resistance suspect. From a nearby cell she overheard German guards interrogating a man. "I heard the most terrifying and hellish sound I have ever heard. . . . It was a man screaming, yelling in long drawn-out agonizing screams, tortured to the breaking point. I could feel myself going white with shock and fear."[3]

The Norwegian underground was so strong the Germans had to keep an army of 300,000 men in the country—men who were desperately needed on other fighting fronts. The Yugoslavian underground, under the guerrilla leader Josip Tito, became a state within a state. In effect, Yugoslavia liberated itself from Nazi rule. In Denmark, boys and girls as young as fourteen served as underground soldiers, setting fire to German supply dumps and disrupting military trains. One of the most powerful of all resistance movements operated behind the fighting fronts in Russia. German truck columns and military trains were under constant attack by the Russian underground. The Germans shot or hung fifty Russian civilians for every German soldier killed behind the lines.

All European underground movements communicated with their countrymen through secret newspapers and magazines. The papers brought news concerning the resistance and stories about German reversals on the front lines. Often the underground press wrote advice on how to sabotage trains and supply trucks. Bold young people riding bicycles delivered the papers, just as they used to deliver traditional newspapers during peacetime. Underground newspapers, however, were carried in secret compartments in a bicycle basket.

The Big Three

"When are you going to start fighting?" Joseph Stalin demanded of Winston Churchill when the two met in Moscow in August 1942. "[After that question] we argued for about two hours," wrote Churchill, "during which time [Stalin] said a great many disagreeable things, especially about our being too much afraid of fighting the Germans."[4]

The angry exchange between Churchill and Stalin illustrates the principal disagreement among the Allied nations in 1942 and 1943. Stalin wanted Britain and the United States to invade France, thereby creating a second front which would take the pressure off the Russian army. The Russian leader believed Italy was a mere sideshow and that his country was being forced to bear the brunt of German might. Certainly Stalin had a point. In 1943 Germany had a four-million-man army in Russia, whereas only 400,000 Germans fought in Italy.

Stalin's desire for a second front was one of many issues dividing the "Big Three"—Stalin, Churchill, and Roosevelt. Some of their disagreements stemmed from personality clashes. Churchill and Stalin openly disliked each other. Roosevelt was a warm friend of Churchill,

The "Big Three" (left to right) Winston Churchill, Franklin D. Roosevelt, and Joseph Stalin pictured at the Yalta conference, February, 1945.

and he claimed he got along well with Stalin. Consequently, Roosevelt often found himself mending fences between the other two Allied leaders.

Roosevelt, Churchill, and Stalin met twice during the war years: at Teheran (in present-day Iran) in 1943, and at Yalta (in what is today the Republic of Ukraine) in 1945. At Teheran, Roosevelt and Churchill promised Stalin a second front, beginning in 1944. At Yalta, when Germany was on the brink of defeat, the Big Three discussed plans for a postwar Europe.

Other Allied war leaders were both a blessing and a bother to the Big Three. Charles de Gaulle was perhaps the most popular French man on earth, but both Churchill and Roosevelt believed him to be vain and power hungry. And in Yugoslavia, no one knew what to make of the resistance leader Josip Tito. Stalin was not sure if Tito was a Communist or a capitalist, and Churchill and Roosevelt wondered if the Yugoslavian strongman would side with the west or with Russia when the war finally ended.

The American Home Front

In the weeks after Pearl Harbor, American industrial plants went through startling changes. Factories that once made cash registers began churning out machine guns. Shops that in peacetime produced typewriter parts shifted to making parts for rifles. The transition from a peacetime to a war economy was achieved swiftly, and the results were miraculous. During the war years, Americans manufactured 87,000 tanks, 2,434,000 trucks, 296,000 planes, 315,000 artillery pieces, and 17,400,000 rifles. No other nation came close to matching the United States in war production. America's frenzied world of buzzing factories and shipyards was called the Home Front.

In addition to outfitting its own army, Home Front workers supplied Great Britain and Russia. Through a program called Lend Lease, $4 billion worth of military gear was sold to Great Britain, and $2 billion to Russia. Bringing Lend Lease goods to Russia was perilous because ships had to sail dangerously near to German airfields and submarine bases in Norway. Still, American goods poured into the Soviet Union. The Studebaker Car Company of South Bend, Indiana, shipped so many trucks to Russia that for a generation after the war, Russians believed the American word for truck was "Studebaker."

Hitler had gambled it would take the United States two years to transport fully equipped armies across the Atlantic. He lost the gamble. By 1945 the U.S. and Britain owned a merchant fleet equal to all the ships in the world in 1939. The leading Allied freight-carrying vessel was the sturdy Liberty Ship, many of which were built by the Kaiser shipyards on America's west coast. During the war, construction time of a Liberty was lowered from thirty weeks to seven weeks. Liberties and other newly-built merchant vessels formed a virtual bridge which channeled goods and troops from the New World to the Old World.

For the American people, life on the Home Front

was a blend of work and worries. Most families had friends or relatives in the military and constantly feared for their safety. Everyone had a demanding work schedule, as a forty-eight-hour week was the norm for factory hands. Children were expected to pitch in to help the war effort. Boys and girls brought bundles of used newspapers to school to be recycled into cartridge cases. Youth groups such as the Boy Scouts and Girl Scouts participated in scrap drives, combing the alleys for discarded cans and other waste metals which were made into bombs and bullets. The words of a popular song went:

> Junk ain't junk no more
> 'Cause junk can win the war.

The frantic demand for factory workers produced new job opportunities for American women. More than six million women took factory jobs during the war years. Many became skilled machinists and mechanics, jobs that were previously denied to women. A fictional character named Rosie the Riveter appeared on posters as a curvaceous young woman, clad in overalls, urging her fellow factory hands to drive more rivets and build more airplanes. Outside the factories, women served for the first time as streetcar conductors and firefighters. In the Pacific Northwest women lumberjacks took to the forests; they were called "lumberjills."

An estimated one million African Americans left the rural south and journeyed to northern big cities to claim factory jobs during the war years. Instead of gainful

The war brought greater job opportunities to women workers on the homefront. These women are repairing track on the B & O railroad, a job that would have been denied them a few years earlier during peacetime.

employment, African Americans frequently found discrimination in jobs and housing. Many factories refused to hire African Americans for anything other than janitorial duties. Federal laws forbade such discrimination, but the factory owners who broke the law usually went unpunished. Because of the discrimination, African-American tempers seethed in the northern industrial cities. On a broiling June night in 1943, a fistfight between black and white youths in Detroit escalated into a riot. When peace was finally restored, twenty-five blacks and nine whites had been killed.

Wartime hysteria drove many Home Front citizens to believe German agents had infiltrated their communities. Strangers in town who spoke with a foreign accent were suspected to have ties with the Nazis. Actually, the Germans attempted to plant saboteurs on American soil only once, in June of 1942, when submarines landed eight English-speaking agents in Florida and on Long Island in New York. The agents had instructions to blow up key bridges and to set fire to aircraft factories. But the would-be saboteurs proved to be rank amateurs. One team of four men spent many of their German-supplied American dollars buying beer in New York City saloons. All eight agents were quickly rounded up by the FBI. *Life* magazine said, "Nothing less than the death penalty [for the saboteurs] will satisfy patriotic Americans."[5] Six of the eight Germans were executed in the electric chair.

Never have soldiers been called upon to endure
longer sustained periods of contact with a vicious
enemy, nor greater punishment from weather or
terrain . . . [We have] conquered them all.
—Dwight D. Eisenhower

Fortress Europe

"If bombs ever fall on Germany," said Hermann Goering, chief of the German Luftwaffe, "then my name is not Goering; it is Meyer." Goering made that famous statement in 1939, when the mighty Luftwaffe ruled the skies above Europe. It contained an element of irony, because Meyer was a common name among German Jews, and no high-ranking Nazi wanted to be mistaken for a Jew. But as the war progressed, British and American bombers began methodically destroying Germany. Goering had to quit visiting cities because angry air raid victims there taunted him with shouts of, "Herr Meyer! Herr Meyer!"

Bombers over Germany

British bombers first raided Berlin on the night of August 24, 1940. The raid did little damage, but the moan of sirens, the ghostly fingers of searchlight beams, and the thudding of bombs terrified the capital's residents.

The British bomber fleet grew in numbers, and on May 30, 1942, its commander, Arthur "Bomber" Harris, put together a 1000-plane raid against the German city of Cologne. Harris believed in area bombing, drenching a whole city with incendiary bombs. The theory behind area bombing was to start fires so great they would eventually spread to the city's industrial regions. On July 24, 1943, "Bomber" Harris, this time with the assistance of American planes, launched a huge raid on Hamburg. Countless tons of incendiary bombs started a firestorm so powerful it sucked in surrounding air from the countryside and created winds strong enough to uproot trees and overturn cars. Hamburg's fire chief called the inferno, "a fire typhoon such as was never before witnessed."

American bombers began to arrive at British bases in January 1942. Pride of the American bomber fleet was the B-17, a four-engine giant that bristled with defensive machine guns. British and American commanders differed on bombing strategies. The British preferred area bombing at night because it was more difficult for German fighter planes to locate bomber groups in the darkness. The Americans believed precision bombing of specific targets during daylight hours would produce

The Boeing B-17 was considered the pride of the American bomber fleet.

more destructive results. American commanders were confident the machine guns of their B-17's would ward off German fighters.

On August 17, 1943, the Americans sent 376 bombers to the cities of Regensburg and Schweinfurt, where the Germans manufactured ball bearings. The raid was a disaster for American flyers. All along the route the B-17's were harassed by Luftwaffe fighter planes. The fighters avoided the mass machine-gun power of the B-17's by attacking the flanks of the formations. When a bomber was hit and began to straggle, the fighters pounced on it, "like wolves on a wounded deer," said an American pilot. The Americans lost sixty bombers on the Schweinfurt mission, and forty-seven other planes returned so badly shot up they had to be junked.

Clearly, the Americans needed fighter aircraft to protect their bombers on daylight missions. But no Allied fighter in 1943 had enough range to make the 1500-mile round trip to Germany. Then a superb plane called the P-51 Mustang appeared in England. A joint American and British development, the single-engine Mustang was swift, nimble, and sufficiently long-range to serve as a bomber escort. Many aviation experts hailed the Mustang as World War II's best fighter. Bomber crews called the planes their "Little Friends."

In 1944 the British continued their night operations while American bombers stepped up their daytime raids. Germany was subjected to terrible round-the-clock bombing. The week of February 19 to 25, 1944, was called "Big Week" by the Allies. In a period of just over

The American P-51 Mustang fighter, a superb long range aircraft.

Essen, like many German cities, was destroyed by bombing attacks.

five days, the Americans put 3,800 bombers over Germany, and the British 2,300. During Big Week the Germans lost 450 fighter planes, most of them to Mustangs. The American air operations commander, Henry "Hap" Arnold, said of Big Week, "Those five days changed the history of the air war."

After Big Week the Allies enjoyed command of the skies. The once proud Luftwaffe was too weakened to stop the relentless round-the-clock bombing. General Adolf Galland, the head of Germany's fighter command, lamented, "The raids on Germany were fatal . . . Hardly a day and rarely a night passed without heavy raids. One German town after another sank into ruin."[1]

One of the most destructive Allied aerial assaults came late in the war and was directed on Dresden in eastern Germany. Dresden was a charming Old World city that had no major war industries. Consequently, it was packed with civilians who moved there believing it to be a safe haven from bombs. The Allies decided to bomb Dresden because they believed the city's destruction would aid the Russian army, which was advancing nearby. The bombing attack began on the night of February 13, 1945, and continued into the next day. German authorities later estimated that 135,000 people died in the horrific firestorm produced by the bombing. A Dresden schoolteacher who survived the nightmare said, "Never would I have thought that death could come to so many people in so many ways . . . burnt, cremated, torn, and crushed to death."

The Road to Rome

Winston Churchill had envisioned Allied troops storming out of their landing areas in Italy and racing toward Rome. But jagged mountains and rushing rivers gave German General Kesselring's defenders a tremendous advantage. Only two main roads led through mountain passes north to Rome. Kesselring concentrated his artillery on the two roadways, thereby nullifying Allied superiority in tanks and trucks. The Italian front became a grinding ordeal where the Allies paid in blood for every yard gained. A famous war correspondent, Ernie Pyle, wrote, "The fighting [in the Italian mountains] sometimes almost reaches the cave man stage. The Americans and the Germans are frequently so close that they actually throw rocks at each other."[2]

Trying to break this deadlock, the Allies landed two divisions behind German lines at Anzio on January 22, 1944. The landings took the Germans by surprise. One American tank driver said, "We came off the ships and marched inland like we were on parade." The Allies were commanded by General John P. Lucas, who was known to be a cautious man. Military historians now believe he was too cautious. Lucas wanted to have ample supplies on the beach before he pushed toward Rome, which lay just thirty-three miles to the north. Instead of sending his troops toward the Italian capital, he put them to work unloading ships. The delay gave the Germans the time they needed to rush reinforcements to the Anzio region. The landing party, which was supposed to be a spearhead, instead became a trapped force.

The inability of the Anzio forces to advance shifted Allied attention back to the main lines. There, the major obstacle barring forward movement was the towering cone-shaped Monte Cassino. Sitting on top of the mountain was a marvelous monastery which dated back to the sixth century. Front line officers believed German observers were using the monastery to direct artillery fire, and they urged that the structure be bombed. At first, higher authorities refused to bomb the building because it was an important religious shrine. Finally the generals gave in to front line demands. On February 15, 1944, the monastery was bombed by a force of 254 planes. In a matter of seconds the great church complex, parts of which had stood for more than one thousand years, was reduced to rubble. It was later discovered the Germans had no artillery spotters in the monastery, and the historic building was destroyed for no good reason.

During the hard winter months on the Italian front, rains drenched Allied soldiers day and night. Foxholes, the only refuge from German shells, filled with icy water. The mud the men lived in was like glue during the day and then turned to iron at night when the temperature dropped below freezing. Fleas infested the soldiers because they had no clean clothes and no place to bathe. Men suffered frostbite and died of pneumonia in muddy holes and caves. Constant rain made the roads so impassable trucks could not evacuate the dead. Corpses lay strewn on the roadsides for days and were sometimes torn open by scavenger dogs.

The spring of 1944, however, produced new

movement in Italy. With incredible effort, tanks and tractors dragged 1,600 heavy guns through the mud and emplaced them at the base of Monte Cassino. The mountain trembled as the guns poured shell after shell at German positions. Slowly, painfully, Allied troops struggled up Monte Cassino's forbidding slopes. The advance was led by Polish soldiers who escaped their country in 1939 to join the Allies. The Poles were hateful and revenge-seeking men, most of whom had lost their families to the German army. They moved up Monte Cassino with cold determination, fighting as if death held little consequence for them. On May 18, 1944, a patrol placed the Polish flag on the peak of Monte Cassino amid the ruins of the historic monastery. Some 4,000 Polish soldiers lost their lives during the advance.

Spring weather allowed the American Fifth Army to cross the Rapido River and make a slow but steady push northward along the Mediterranean coast. In late May, advance elements of the Fifth Army linked up with the Anzio front. Now the Americans turned toward their ultimate goal—Rome. General Mark Clark, the commander of the Fifth Army, entered Rome on June 5, 1944. "There were gay crowds on the streets," he wrote. "Flowers were stuck in the muzzles of soldiers' rifles. Many Romans seemed to be on the verge of hysteria for the American troops."

The liberation of Rome made headlines for only one day because world attention was quickly drawn to Normandy, a coastal region in France where the largest amphibious invasion in military history had just begun.

An American 240mm howitzer, one of the heaviest guns in the American arsenal, fires shells into German positions in Italy.

D-Day

It was a fleet so large its sight left even veteran sailors awestruck. Some four thousand vessels—from 30,000-ton battleships to craft the size of pleasure boats—bobbed in the waves off the Normandy coast. Landing boats in this massive fleet carried 200,000 soldiers. It was D-Day, June 6, 1944, the long-awaited date for an Allied invasion of Europe.

Hours earlier, during the night of June 5, a huge formation of transport aircraft dropped 13,000 paratroopers behind the Normandy landing beaches. The airborne soldiers were ordered to destroy strong points and to repel German counterattacks. But because of pilot error, many units landed in the wrong areas. Some parachuted into swamps where men, burdened by heavy packs, drowned in less than two feet of water. At least one plane load of paratroopers jumped directly into the English Channel, and the men were swallowed up by the sea. Still other paratroopers dropped so near German positions they were machine-gunned while dangling from their parachute straps.

On the British coast, American General Dwight Eisenhower paced the floor of his headquarters. Eisenhower, the future American president, was in charge of the D-Day operation. Now he worried as he heard the reports of confusion and heavy casualties suffered by the airborne troops. He later said that during D-Day he and his staff felt, "as tense as a coiled spring."

Guns from hundreds of warships blasted German fortifications at Normandy. The entire shoreline erupted

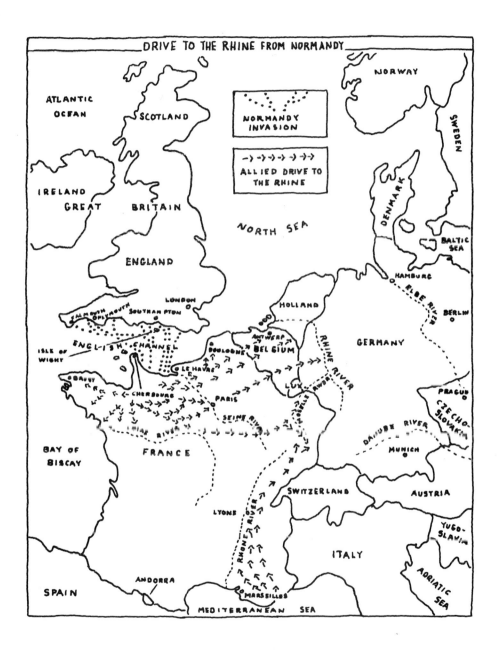

DRIVE TO THE RHINE FROM NORMANDY

NORMANDY
INVASION

-) -) -) -) -) -)
ALLIED DRIVE TO
THE RHINE

ATLANTIC
OCEAN

NORWAY

SCOTLAND

SWEDEN

IRELAND
GREAT BRITAIN

NORTH SEA

DENMARK

BALTIC
SEA

ENGLAND

HAMBURG

ELBE RIVER

BERLIN

LONDON

HOLLAND

FALMOUTH
PLYMOUTH SOUTHAMPTON

ANTWERP

GERMANY

ENGLISH CHANNEL

BELGIUM

RHINE RIVER

ISLE OF
WIGHT

BOULOGNE

PRAGUE

BREST

LE HAVRE

LUX.

CZECHO-
SLOVAKIA

CHERBOURG

PARIS

DANUBE RIVER

SEINE RIVER

MUNICH

BAY OF
BISCAY

LOIRE RIVER

FRANCE

SWITZERLAND

AUSTRIA

LYONS

YUGO-
SLAVIA

RHONE RIVER

ITALY

ADRIATIC
SEA

SPAIN

ANDORRA

MARSEILLES

MEDITERRANEAN SEA

General Dwight Eisenhower, commander of the D-Day operations.

in fire and smoke. While the shells screamed overhead, wave after wave of landing craft churned toward the beaches. The men packed inside the tiny boats were wet, cold, and miserably seasick. They had bounced about in the choppy seas for more than twenty-four hours. On some boats the decks were slimy with vomit.

At 6:30 A.M. soldiers assaulted the Normandy coastline at five points. Hell rained at a beach code-named Omaha. From the cliffs and bluffs overlooking Omaha, the Germans opened fire with their devilishly accurate 88mm guns. Many boats were blown apart while they were still hundreds of yards from shore. Other landing craft became hung up on sandbars, forcing the men to jump into chest-high water and wade ashore in the teeth of whistling machine-gun fire. The beaches became strewn with bodies and parts of bodies. Newspaper writers called this terrible beachhead "Bloody Omaha."

Commander of German defense forces was General Irwin Rommel, the famed desert fox. "The enemy's entire landing operation must under no circumstances be allowed to last longer than a matter of hours, or at the most, days," Rommel told his superiors in Berlin.[3] He knew from bitter experience that Allied supremacy in the air meant the German army could not freely move tanks and trucks to challenge a foe. Therefore, the invaders must be gunned down on the beaches by well-protected troops. To accomplish this, Rommel built an elaborate system of tunnels and artillery emplacements along the beachlines. German propaganda ministers called his defensive network "the Atlantic Wall," or "Fortress

American soldiers land on the coast of France during D-Day, June 6, 1944.

An American medic who served wounded soldiers on D-Day, June 6, 1944.

Europe." But Rommel knew his Atlantic Wall had naked gaps because it was impossible to fortify every potential landing area. He had no idea when or where the Allies would strike.

With the exception of the carnage at Omaha Beach, the Allies pushed inland at all Normandy fronts. On D-Day afternoon, a patrol of the American Fourth Infantry Division linked up with paratroopers behind Utah Beach. The meeting between airborne and ground troops meant the initial stage of the D-Day operation had met its aims. Late that evening, a gloomy General Rommel listened to invasion reports over the telephone. June 6 was his wife's birthday, and he had gone home to Germany to celebrate with his family. It was his last family gathering. Rommel, who desperately wanted to end the war, was implicated in a June, 1944 plot to kill Hitler, and he was forced to commit suicide by taking poison.

The Russian War Machine

"Hitlerite Germany and her army have been shaken, but they have not been stopped as yet," said the Soviet leader Joseph Stalin in May of 1943. "Another two or three powerful blows are needed for the catastrophe of Hitlerite Germany to be an accomplished fact."[4]

Certainly one of the blows Stalin hoped to deliver against Hitler was the battle shaping up near the central Russian city of Kursk. It was a conflict German commanders entered reluctantly. Since the slaughter at Stalingrad, German generals had wanted to fight a defensive war in Russia until they could rebuild their tank forces. But Hitler insisted his armies take the offense. The Fuhrer hoped his new tanks—the Tiger and the Panther—would rout the Russians. The Tiger was a giant machine, weighing fifty-six tons and armed with the feared 88mm gun. The Panther was a fast and powerful medium tank, built to outclass the Russian T-34. However, both these tanks broke down often due to mechanical problems, and German commanders had precious few of the new machines. By contrast, factories in the Soviet Union were churning out more than 1,000 dependable T-34's each month.

The attack began on July 5, 1943, with hordes of German tanks roaring over the farmland near Kursk. The Germans did not know they were racing into a trap. Information concerning the German offensive had fallen into Russian hands, and Soviet commanders massed their artillery at the area where they knew the enemy would strike. The German tanks were hit by a savage storm of gunfire. "The Russian artillery plowed the earth around us," said the driver of a Tiger tank. "The whole front was a girdle of flashes. It seemed as if we were driving into a rain of fire."

The Russian commander, Georgi Zhukov, was an energetic, barrel-chested man who seemed to be everywhere all at once. Riding a light truck he raced among the ranks of tank and artillery men, urging them to kill the Nazi invaders. Early in the war his fellow officers considered Zhukov to be a hesitant commander, but he grew more willing to take risks as he rolled up victories.

Years later he wrote about the earthshaking artillery barrage his men hurled at the German armor assaulting Kursk: "I could hear and sense the hurricane of fire, and I could well picture the plight of the enemy struck down by the violent fire."

The Battle of Kursk raged for eight days. Altogether it involved more than two million men and six thousand tanks, making it the biggest clash of armor in world history. Battle lines disappeared as both sides sent waves of armored vehicles rumbling at each other. Smoke and dust kicked up by the iron giants blanketed the battlefield, adding to the terror and the confusion. "It was hard to tell who was attacking and who was defending," said a Russian officer. Finally the German commanders were forced to withdraw from Kursk, after having lost half their tanks and suffering 90,000 casualties. Heinz Guderian, Germany's most respected tank commander, wrote, "[After Kursk] there were to be no more periods of quiet on the eastern front. From now on the enemy was in undisputed possessions of the initiative."[5]

Far to the north, a Soviet city under siege reawakened. Leningrad had been surrounded since the German offensive in 1941. Starving city dwellers at first ate their dogs and cats. Later they were reduced to making soups out of glue and wallpaper paste. An estimated one million Leningraders—about one out of every three residents—died during the two and one-half years the city was surrounded. A survivor of the Leningrad ordeal, Vera Inver, wrote, "There are many coffins to be seen in the streets. They are transported on sleighs. . . . Recently

I saw a body without a coffin. It had on its chest some wood shavings, apparently as a mark of dignity."[6]

In January 1944 the Russian army began a winter offensive near Leningrad. Soldiers brought up Katyusha rocket-launchers, which fired deadly projectiles in waves and created vast killing fields on the ground. Because of the horrible screaming sound they made, German infantrymen called the Katyusha rockets "Stalin's pipe organs." By the end of January the Germans had been pushed from the outskirts of Leningrad. No longer could their heavy guns shell the city. For the first time in what seemed to be an eternity, Leningraders stepped into their streets and enjoyed silence and freedom from shell fire. One woman, gazing upon the ruined but suddenly tranquil city, wrote, "Leningrad emerged from the gloom before our eyes."

By mid-1944 Russian tanks and infantry units were driving steadily towards Germany's eastern borders. The landings in Normandy, to Germany's west, had created the second front that was long desired by Russian leaders. The Nazi nation was now caught in the jaws of a vice that its once mighty war machine could not stop from closing.

Use steam roller strategy; that is, make up your mind on the course and direction of action and stick to it.
—General George S. Patton

Victory

The Allied successes in 1944 cast a cloud of gloom over Berlin, but fanatical Nazis insisted their amazing new armaments would still win the war. The revolutionary German devices were called *Vergeltungswaffen,* "Vengeance weapons," or simply V weapons. They were intended to avenge the Allies for the bombing raids and the miseries they heaped upon Germany.

The Wonder Weapons

Just ten days after D-Day, the Germans employed the first of their V weapons, a jet-propelled flying bomb called the V-1. Carrying an explosive charge of more than 2,000 pounds, the V-1 was launched from bases in France and Belgium and aimed usually at London. It was a terror weapon, made to kill and frighten civilians. In flight, the V-1 made a fearful buzzing sound. Londoners called it the "buzz bomb." More than 9,000 V-1's were fired against England, but only 5,000 crashed near their target. The buzz bombs flew at just over 300 mph, and many were shot out of the sky by fighter planes or were brought down by antiaircraft fire.

A far more menacing weapon was the V-2, a rocket-propelled ballistic missile which weighed almost fourteen tons. When fired, the V-2 arched fifty miles into the sky before plunging on its target. It was impossible to shoot down in flight, and since it flew at more than four times the speed of sound, people on the ground were unable to hear it approach. The first V-2's were sent into the air in September 1944. Before the end of the war, about 1,100 V-2's were fired at English targets, resulting in 2,700 deaths and many thousands of injuries.

Both the V-1 and the V-2 were developed at a scientific center in the German city of Peenemunde. One of the leading Peenemunde scientists was Wernher von Braun, who, after the war, helped the United States develop rockets for its space program. Before the first V weapons were produced, Allied spies learned of the work at Peenemunde, and bombers made a major air strike there in August 1943. The air raid damaged precious equipment and killed several key scientists. Because of the raid, development of the V-1 and the V-2 was set back at least five months, and the delay helped the Allied cause immeasurably. After the war American and British generals admitted it would have been difficult to go

A dreaded V-1 "buzz bomb" in flight.

forward with the D-Day operations if V-1 and V-2 bombs were raining out of the skies on their assembly areas in England.

A weapon with even greater potential to turn the course of the war was a jet fighter plane called the ME 262. Germany was a world leader in jet propulsion. In 1939 the German Heinkel Company flew the first air-breathing jet aircraft. Three years later, German engineers completed a test version of the ME 262. In addition to its jet engine, the new fighter had revolutionary swept-back wings. Production models reached the unheard-of speed of 540 mph, and the new plane was able to fly higher than any Allied aircraft. But when Hitler first saw this highly advanced fighter he blurted out, "Can this plane drop bombs?" He then became obsessed with the idea of bombing England with a fleet of jets too swift to be intercepted by Allied fighters. At Hitler's orders, production of the ME 262 was held back while attempts were made to build a jet-propelled bomber. The bomber never became operational, and because of the delays the ME 262 fighter was not mass-produced until the closing months of 1944—too late to have an impact on Allied air supremacy.

German science developed other wonder weapons which would certainly have made an impact on the war had they been produced earlier and in greater numbers. The Luftwaffe built a small rocket plane designed to shoot down bombers which flew even faster than their jets. German scientists fashioned an air-launched antiaircraft missile which homed in on enemy airplanes by

The highly advanced German ME 262 jet fighter, capable of flying
at 540 mph.

seeking out the heat produced by their piston engines. A ground-launched antiaircraft missile called the Waterfall was guided to its target by radar and carried an explosive charge which weighed almost 700 pounds. Years after the war, Hitler's chief aide, Albert Speer, wrote, "To this day I think [the Waterfall] rocket, in conjunction with the jet fighter, would have beaten back the western Allies from the spring of 1944 on."[1]

Futuristic weapons were also made for the German submarine fleet. A tube device the Germans called the Snorkel allowed their subs to stay submerged while taking in air needed to run their diesel engines. A new submarine, the type XXI, was built. It was twice the size of existing German submarines, and its streamlined hull gave it far greater speed. The Germans armed the sub with a deadly torpedo that sought out the sound of enemy propellers and could hit a ship, even if it sailed on a zigzag course.

The Allies too rushed to develop special weapons which they hoped would hasten victory. Among their devices was a radio-controlled guided bomb that had a bright flare burning at its tail section. The flare allowed an operator in an airplane to direct the bomb, through radio signals, to strike a key target such as a bridge or an important factory. The radio-controlled bomb was an early example of a guided missile. Another Allied invention was an inflatable flotation device which surrounded a tank allowing it to "swim" across a river. Perhaps the most successful Allied secret weapon was the proximity fuse—a tiny radar set placed inside an artillery or an

A German U-boat under attack by the U.S.S *Bogue.*

antiaircraft shell. The radar set directed the shell to burst when it came near an airplane or the ground, eliminating the need for complex timing fuses. Artillery shells with proximity fuses were used late in the war against German infantry with devastating effects.

The Second Front

In less than three weeks after D-Day, more than one million men had embarked on beaches in France. But a dramatic offensive in northern France was hampered by a maze of hedgerows. Hedgerows were low fences made from rocks and tangles of brush that French farmers cleared from their fields. The fences provided perfect cover for German riflemen and machine guns. The journalist A. J. Liebling, who traveled with the American army through hedgerow country, wrote,

> The Germans dig behind the hedgerows like moles—moles with excellent eyesight—and the pattern of the fields gives them a fine opportunity for crossfire . . . The business of routing them out of the fields is both dangerous and tedious . . . You don't know where an enemy position is until a machine gun opens fire on you.[2]

Far to the south another amphibious assault on France took place. On August 15, 1944, a fleet of 1,500 ships, including several aircraft carriers, landed an Allied army on the French Mediterranean coast near the city of Cannes. The landings were almost uncontested, and they created a southern front. In just one month the southern front linked with the D-Day invaders to the north, giving the Allies a battle line that stretched the length of France.

Street fighting in Paris.

Turmoil seized Paris as the Allies pushed close to its outskirts. Hitler ordered the city to be burned rather than handed over to the enemy. But German commanders refused to wantonly destroy Paris, one of Europe's most beautiful cities. Instead, the main force of Germans withdrew, leaving Paris undamaged. On August 26, 1944, General Charles de Gaulle marched triumphantly into the French capital and Parisians went wild in celebration. The festivities turned deadly, however, when die-hard German snipers fired at crowds from rooftops. Confusion and terror reigned. In some neighborhoods people danced in the streets while just a few blocks away others cowered from rifle shots.

In the countryside east of Paris, the fiery General George Patton drove his Third Army towards Germany. Patton had a strange, almost lustful zeal for war and risk-taking. As a young cadet at West Point he once poked his head into the line of fire at the rifle range just so he could experience danger firsthand. His outspoken remarks and tough actions often got him in trouble with Eisenhower and with the American press. At a front line hospital in 1943 he slapped a soldier in the face and called him yellow because the man said he was suffering from combat fatigue rather than a physical illness. The slapping incident temporarily cost Patton his field command. He was returned to combat after D-Day to lead the drive into Germany.

Allied armies reached the Belgian border in September, 1944. To speed the Allied advance, Eisenhower approved a daring plan offered by British General

Montgomery. The plan called for a giant airborne operation involving 4,500 planes and gliders to land troops
behind enemy lines and take key bridges in Holland.
Eisenhower hoped the airborne operation would ease the
capture of Antwerp, an important port and a base from
which the Germans were firing V-2's at Great Britain.
The parachute drop, however, was a near disaster. The
British First Airborne Division landed in the heart of
German defenses and suffered enormous casualties. Antwerp finally fell into Allied hands, but only after terrible
loss of life.

The Battle of the Bulge

In the autumn of 1944, Adolf Hitler made plans for a
surprise offensive designed to rescue his country from
defeat. The offensive was his pet idea, and he hoped its
results would be earthshaking. The Nazi leader in-
structed his generals to scrape together every possible
military unit and strike the Allies through the Ardennes
Forest in the Belgian and Luxembourg region. To Hitler
there was magic in the Ardennes, the site of the 1940
glorious blitzkrieg.

Following Hitler's instructions, more than 300,000
German troops and hundreds of tanks assembled secretly
in the Ardennes. Hitler ordered the men to penetrate
American positions and drive toward Antwerp. The German leader believed the pact between Russia and the
western powers was weak. He hoped the capture of Antwerp would diminish the resolve of Britain and America
and encourage them to make a separate peace with

Germany. Then he could shift all of Germany's resources to the east and stop the Russian advance. It was a desperate plan, conceived by a desperate mind.

The Ardennes front was quiet in December 1944. A gentle snow fell, decorating the pine trees and making American troops think of Christmas. Then, in the early morning darkness of December 16, the Ardennes erupted with explosions. A hellish German artillery barrage rattled the forest for an hour, although it seemed like an eternity in terror for the GI's huddled in foxholes. When the shelling lifted, American soldiers heard the distinctive clanging of tank treads. Out of the forest came waves of huge German tanks. The giant machines were followed by crouching infantrymen, most of them dressed in white cloaks as camouflage against the snow-covered ground.

American officers were astounded. They thought the German army was far too weak to launch a major offensive. But now tanks and troops drove forward with determination, as they once did in the blitzkriegs of old. In practically every sector of the Ardennes front, officers ordered a retreat. In American headquarters an ominous black bulge representing German gains grew on the operations map. Consequently the German attack has forever been called the Battle of the Bulge.

Not content with conducting a pure military offensive, the Germans also employed a special force of commandos who pierced the battle lines and spread confusion in the rear areas. The commandos spoke English and wore American uniforms. One team of infiltrators,

American troops in the snowy Ardennes forest during the Battle of the Bulge.

riding in a captured jeep, twisted a sign at a crossroads and sent scores of trucks bearing American infantrymen away from instead of towards the front lines. Another commando group blocked a key road by putting up warning signs in English announcing the roadway was heavily mined.

Only about 150 German commandos infiltrated American ranks, but their mere presence spread panic. After several teams were captured, rumor spread from GI to GI that English-speaking German infiltrators were everywhere. The Americans were unable to tell friend from foe. In the rear areas men were forced at rifle point to prove they were Americans. High-ranking officers and soldiers on important missions were halted and questioned about aspects of American life: Who is Mickey Mouse's girlfriend? Name Donald Duck's three nephews. General Omar Bradley's jeep was stopped by a soldier who demanded to know the capital of Illinois. Bradley answered, correctly, Springfield. The soldier blurted out, "You're wrong; it's Chicago."

One of the bloodiest episodes of the Battle of the Bulge took place at a small town in Belgium called Bastone. The town was defended by elements of the American 101st Airborne Division commanded by General Anthony McAuliffe. On the morning of December 22, four German officers carrying a white flag approached a Bastone road block. The Germans were taken to headquarters, where they presented a note to General McAuliffe. The note read: "The fortune of war is changing. This time U.S.A. forces have been encircled by strong German armored units . . ." The note demanded the Americans surrender immediately.

It was true the men of the 101st were surrounded at Bastone, but General McAuliffe was confident American units would soon come to his rescue. He took the German note and scratched out a now famous reply:

> To the German Commander
> NUTS!
> The American Commander.

On December 23, 1944 the thick fog which had hung over the Ardennes region for days lifted, and transport planes parachuted supplies to the trapped men at Bastone. Air-dropped supplies allowed American units in the entire Ardennes region to stop the German advance. The weather then turned bitterly cold, and both sides suffered thousands of frostbite cases. Wounded men froze to death in their foxholes. Battling through heavy snows, General Patton led an armored column into the Ardennes region to break the German offensive. By January 16, 1945, a month after Hitler launched the attack, the Ardennes front had collapsed to about the same position it had been in thirty days earlier. Thousands of German troops had died, but the Nazi nation gained nothing. The last blitzkrieg of World War II sputtered and died in the snowy Ardennes Forest.

Just after the Battle of the Bulge the Big Three—Roosevelt, Churchill, and Stalin—met at Yalta in the Soviet Republic of the Ukraine. At the meeting Stalin agreed to enter the war against Japan within three months of Germany's defeat. Churchill was forced to concede that much of eastern Europe would fall under Russian domination at war's end. Ironies are always present in the politics of war. In 1939 Britain went to war to defend Poland from Hitler's aggression; in 1945, at Yalta, Churchill virtually surrendered Poland to Stalin.

The Fall of Germany

Germany's Rhine River is gently flowing and over the centuries has inspired musical pieces and poetry. But in 1945 it loomed as a potentially bloody military barrier for the Allies. As Allied infantry approached the Rhine, German engineers blew up its bridges, and troops dug in on its eastern banks. Crossing this broad river would surely be a nightmare for Allied forces. Then, on March 17, 1945, American GI's approaching the river near the town of Remagen spotted a miracle—a railroad bridge which the Germans had somehow failed to blow up. Dodging enemy fire, the Americans raced to the other side of the bridge. They discovered the bridge was wired with explosives, but the Germans had yet to pull the switch. The taking of the bridge at Remagen was an incredible fortune of war for the Allies. To the Germans it was a disaster. One German general said, "Never in the war was there more concentrated bad luck than at Remagen."

After they pierced the Rhine, the western Allies were an unstoppable force. The German defenders seemed powerless to even slow down their advance. A *Life* magazine correspondent, who traveled with an American unit, wrote, "The German Army, disorganized by the speed of

An American and a Russian soldier meet on the battlefield on April 25, 1945. The historic meeting meant Germany was cut in two by the Allied forces.

the Allied rush across the Rhine, began to make mistakes like a boxer who has been hit on the head too often."[3] Capturing German territory at the rate of almost forty miles a day, the Americans, the British, and the free French created their own version of blitzkrieg. A great encircling movement in the Ruhr Valley surrounded more than 300,000 German soldiers. The Ruhr was also Germany's industrial hub. Its seizure was a death blow to Nazi war production.

On the morning of April 12, 1945, American President Franklin Roosevelt said, "I have a terrific headache." He then collapsed and died. In Berlin Hitler was overjoyed. He believed Roosevelt's sudden death would somehow reverse the course of the war. "Here we have a miracle," he shouted to one of his aides. "The war isn't lost! Roosevelt is dead!" But in the closing weeks Hitler had lost all sense of reason. By the spring of 1945 the Nazi government's fate had long been sealed in defeat. Nothing—certainly not the sudden death of the American president—could save Germany.

History was made on April 25, 1945, along the banks of the Ebbe River, some seventy-five miles south of Berlin, when advance elements of the American infantry met with a Russian patrol. Germany was now cut in two. The Americans and the Russians knew victory was near. To celebrate the historic linkup, a band was called to the front, and Russian and American soldiers danced together. Above the makeshift dance floor someone hung pictures of Stalin and Roosevelt. Roosevelt had died suddenly two weeks earlier, but no one in the front lines had a picture of the new president, Harry S. Truman.

In Berlin the last large battle of the European war raged as hordes of Russian infantry, accompanied by tanks, swarmed into the city. Women, children, and the elderly trembled in basements while furious combat erupted in the streets. Many Russian troops went wild in conquest—killing civilians, looting, and raping women.

In the center of the tortured city, Adolf Hitler directed Germany's last stand from a room in his thick-walled bunker. His aide, Albert Speer, saw him several times in the bunker while Berlin collapsed around him. "He was shriveling up like an old man," Speer wrote. "His limbs trembled; he walked stooped, with dragging footsteps. Even his voice became quavering and lost its old masterfulness . . . When he talked about the end he meant his own and not that of the nation."[4]

On April 30, 1945, Hitler committed suicide by placing a pistol in his mouth and pulling the trigger. His wife, Eva Braun, joined him in death by taking poison. He had married Eva only hours before their death. The day after the twin suicides, Berlin radio announced that Adolf Hitler, the World War I veteran, was killed in the streets of Berlin while battling Russian invaders. In the early morning of May 7, 1945, General Alfred Jodl offered Germany's unconditional surrender to the Allies. After five years and eight months, the European War came to an end.

It is not so difficult to keep unity in time of war, since there is a joint aim to defeat the common enemy, which is clear to everyone. The difficult time will come after the war, when diverse interests tend to divide the allies.
　　—Joseph Stalin

7 The Aftermath

"It was like no other day that anyone can remember," said the writer Mollie Panter-Downes, reporting from London as the people celebrated V-E Day (Victory in Europe). "Crowds milled back and forth between Buckingham Palace, Trafalgar Square, and Piccadilly Circus. . . . One small boy holding onto his father's hand [asked about the air raid shelters]. 'You'll never have to use the shelters again, son.' 'Never?' the child asked doubtfully. 'Never!' the man cried almost angrily. '*Never*! Understand?' "[1]

Hitler was dead and the Nazi evil erased from the earth. Only now, in the smoking ruins of Germany and in what was once Nazi-occupied Europe, were the depths of Nazi atrocities beginning to be understood.

American servicemen and British civilians celebrate V-E Day on the streets of London.

Allied armies overrunning Germany and eastern Europe opened the gates of the dreaded death camps and uncovered conditions so cruel they sickened even battle-hardened soldiers. Behind the barbed wire the Allies found prisoners so ravaged by hunger they looked like skin stretched over skeletons. The dead were everywhere, buried in mass graves, or stacked like logs because there were too many to bury. Looking at one tangle of bodies, an American officer wrote,

> [The dead] were so thin and dried out that they might have been plaster of Paris, and you had to keep saying to yourself, these were human beings, and when you said it your mind was not believing it, because nothing like this had ever happened before and it just couldn't happen.

The victorious Allied nations agreed the leaders of Germany had to be punished for committing these terrible crimes. Trials of key Nazi figures were held in the German city of Nuremberg from 1945 to 1949. German leaders, including Hermann Goering, were accused of murder, enslavement, and the persecution of Jews and other racial minorities. Many of the Germans offered the defense, "I was just following orders." The court refused to accept this argument, and sentenced the offenders to prison terms or to death by hanging. On October 16, 1946, ten of the most powerful Nazis tried at Nuremberg were hung. Hermann Goering cheated the rope by committing suicide hours before his scheduled execution. To this day no one knows how the

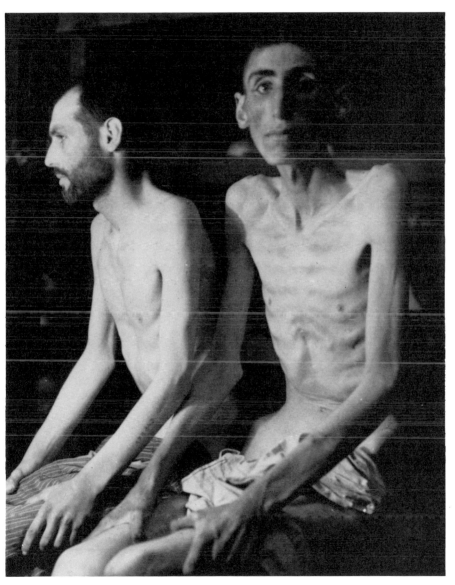

Inmates at a German camp. These men worked as slave laborers and because of a starvation diet their weight dropped to 70 pounds or less.

closely guarded Goering obtained the cyanide tablet which he swallowed to take his life.

Aside from the need to punish ex-Nazis, Allied leaders agreed on few other postwar programs. The fall of Germany created a sea of problems. Russia was now the supreme power in Europe. As the continent's dominant nation, Russia imposed Communist governments in Poland, Rumania, Bulgaria, Czechoslovakia, and other Eastern European countries. Those nations became satellite states, puppet governments controlled by Moscow. Germany was divided into occupied zones by the Allies. The divisions eventually gave rise to two new states: East Germany and West Germany. In the decades following the war, East Germany had a Communist government, and West Germany a capitalistic system.

The splintering of Europe into Communist and non-Communist camps was a symptom of the Cold War, a period of tension between Russia and the West which lasted more than forty years. A famous 1946 speech by Winston Churchill spelled out the perilous state of the Cold War world: "From Stettin in the Baltic to Trieste in the Adriatic, an iron curtain has descended across the [European] continent." The Cold War dissolved in the late 1980s and early 1990s with the breakup of the Soviet Union, the reunification of Germany, and the overthrow of Communism in the Iron Curtain countries.

In early May 1945 the Cold War with all its uncertainties and fears were future prospects which could not dim the celebration of V-E Day. True, the Pacific War

A grizzly scene at a German death camp. This picture shows less than half the bodies discovered at the camp.

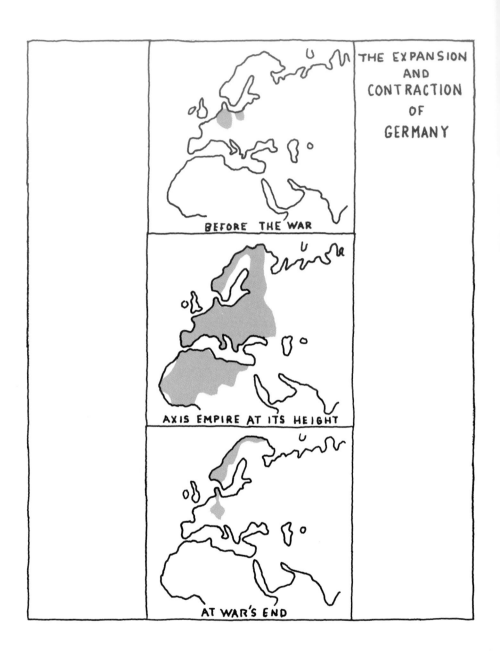

THE EXPANSION
AND
CONTRACTION
OF
GERMANY

BEFORE THE WAR

AXIS EMPIRE AT ITS HEIGHT

AT WAR'S END

was still being fought with a cruel fury. While Allied peoples rejoiced over V-E Day, a terrible battle raged on Okinawa, a large island just south of Japan. The Allies suffered almost 50,000 casualties in their efforts to take Okinawa from fanatical Japanese defenders. Still, the people celebrated the fact that at least one powerful enemy—Nazi Germany—had been eliminated. In Paris, church bells rang and Parisians sang in the streets. In Moscow, a dazzling fireworks display lit the night sky. In New York, radio stations broadcast triumphant music to every American town and village. In London, a cautious Winston Churchill reminded the British people of their still formidable Japanese enemy when he ended his victory message with the words: "I told you hard things at [the beginning of the war], and I should be unworthy of your confidence and generosity if I still did not cry: Forward, unflinching, unswerving, indomitable, till the whole task is done and the whole world is safe and clean."

Chronology

January 30, 1933—After the Nazi Party won 40 percent of the vote in a 1932 election, President Paul von Hindenburg named Adolf Hitler chancellor (prime minister) of Germany.

August 2, 1934—President von Hindenburg died; Hitler proclaimed himself the ruler of Germany.

March 7, 1936—At Hitler's orders, the German army marched into the Rhineland, a region on the border with France; the move was a violation of the Versailles Treaty drawn up at the end of World War I.

March 12, 1938—Hitler sent his armies into Austria and made that country part of greater Germany.

September 29, 1938—Britain and France agreed to give the Sudetenland, a region of Czechoslovakia, to Germany.

September 1, 1939—Germany invaded Poland.

September 3, 1939—Britain and France declared war on Germany.

September 17, 1939—Russia attacked Poland from the east.

September 27, 1939—Warsaw, the Polish capital, surrendered to Germany.

April 9, 1940—Germany invaded Denmark and Norway.

May 10, 1940—In order to outflank France's powerful Maginot Line, Germany invaded the neutral countries of Belgium, Luxembourg, and the Netherlands.

May 28, 1940—The Belgium army surrendered leaving a large force of British and French troops trapped at Dunkirk; the British begin a heroic rescue operation.

June 10, 1940—Italy declared war on France.

August 13, 1940—The German Luftwaffe made a massive air raid on British airfields; the Battle of Britain began.

August 24, 1940—The British air force (RAF) made its first raid on Berlin.

February 12, 1941—German general Irwin Rommel arrived in North Africa; the desert war started between the British and Rommel's Africa Corps.

April 6, 1941—Germany attacked Yugoslavia and Greece.

June 22, 1941—Germany invaded Russia.

December 7, 1941—Japan launched a surprise attack on the American naval base at Pearl Harbor in Hawaii.

December 11, 1941—Hitler, claiming solidarity with Japan, declared war on America.

May 30, 1942—The RAF raided the German city of Cologne with a force of 1,000 bombers.

June 22, 1942—Rommel's Africa Corps captured Tobruk, an important British stronghold.

August 7, 1942—Winston Churchill named British general Bernard Montgomery to command the forces in Africa.

September 16, 1942—The German army entered the Soviet city of Stalingrad.

October 23, 1942—The British began an offense at El Alamein in North Africa.

November 7-8, 1942—American troops landed in North Africa.

November 19, 1942—The Russians began a counterattack at Stalingrad.

January 31, 1943—German general Paulus surrendered at Stalingrad; the Germans lost about 300,000 men killed or captured during the battle.

February 20-21, 1943—American troops suffered heavy casualties at the Kasserine Pass in North Africa.

May 13, 1943—The Africa Corps surrendered to the Allies; General Rommel escaped to Germany.

July 5, 1943—The Battle of Kursk began in central Russia.

July 10, 1943—Allies invaded Sicily.

July 24, 1943—British and American bombers set in motion a huge air raid on the German city of Hamburg.

August 17, 1943—American bombers experienced great losses during a raid on Schweinfurt.

September 3, 1943—The Allies landed in Italy.

January 22, 1944—Allied troops landed at Anzio in Italy.

January 27, 1944—The Russians began an offensive in the Leningrad area.

February 19-25, 1944—The British and Americans launched a series of air raids on German targets in an operation called Big Week.

May 18, 1944—Allied soldiers took Monte Cassino in Italy.

June 5, 1944—The Allies marched into Rome.

June 6, 1944—D-Day, the greatest amphibious operation in history, took place at Normandy in France.

August 15, 1944—Allied troops land in southern France.

August 26, 1944—Paris was liberated.

December 16, 1944—The Battle of the Bulge began when Germany launched a surprise offensive.

January 16, 1945—The Battle of the Bulge ended with no German gains.

February 4, 1945—A conference began at Yalta where Roosevelt, Churchill, and Stalin met to discuss postwar plans.

February 13, 1945—A terrible fire bombing on Dresden destroyed the city; the Germans claimed 135,000 civilians were killed in the raid.

March 17, 1945—American troops captured the Rhine River bridge at the city of Remagen.

April 12, 1945—Roosevelt dies suddenly.

April 22, 1945—American and Russian soldiers met at the Ebbe River; Germany is now cut in two.

April 30, 1945—Hitler committed suicide in his Berlin bunker.

May 7, 1945—Germany surrendered to the Allies.

August 6, 1945—A B-29 drops a single atomic bomb on Hiroshima; at least 80,000 people were killed by the blast.

August 8, 1945—Russia declares war on Japan.

August 9, 1945—An atomic bomb is dropped on Nagasaki.

August 14, 1945—Japan surrenders to the Allies.

September 2, 1945—The official surrender documents are signed in a ceremony on board the U.S.S. *Missouri*, docked in Tokyo Bay.

Notes by Chapter

Chapter One

1. Shirer, William L. *Berlin Diary: The Journal of a Foreign Correspondent.* New York: Bonanza Books, 1984, p191.

Chapter Two

1. Churchill, Winston. *The Second World War* Vol. 2 *Their Finest Hour.* Boston: Houghton Mifflin Co., 1949, p226.

2. Murrow, Edward R. *This Is London.* New York: Simon and Schuster, 1941, p171.

3. Westall, Robert (editor). *Children of the Blitz: Memories of Wartime Childhood.* New York: Viking, 1985, p104.

4. Churchill, Winston. *The Second World War* Vol. 2 *Their Finest Hour.* Boston: Houghton Mifflin Co., 1949, p598.

5. Westall, Robert (editor). *Children of the Blitz: Memories of Wartime Childhood.* New York: Viking, 1985, p112.

6. Guderian, Heinz. *Panzer Leader.* New York: Ballantine Books, 1957, pp182-83.

Chapter Three

1. Martin, Ralph. *The GI War 1941-45*. Boston: Little, Brown & Co., 1967, p44.

2. Rommel, Erwin (edited by Liddell Hart). *The Rommel Papers*. New York: Harcourt Brace, 1953, p398.

3. Speech by Winston Churchill delivered in London on Lord Mayor's Day, November 10, 1942.

4. Sulzberger, C.L. *The American Heritage History of World War II* (Eyewitness section). New York: American Heritage Publishing Company, 1966, p273.

Chapter Four

1. Speer, Albert. *Inside the Third Reich*. New York: The Macmillan Company, 1969, p65.

2. Frank, Anne. *Diary of a Young Girl*. New York: Doubleday, 1961 (20th printing), p58.

3. Hunt, Antonia. *Little Resistance, A Teenage English Girl's Adventures in Occupied France*. New York: St. Martin's Press, 1982, p109.

4. Churchill, Winston. *The Second World War* Vol. 4 *Hinge of Fate*. Boston: Houghton Mifflin Co., 1949, p486.

5. *Life* magazine. July 3, 1942, p33.

Chapter Five

1. Galland, Adolf. *The First and the Last*. New York: Henry Holt & Co., 1954, p287.

2. Pyle, Ernie (David Nichols, editor). *Ernie's War,*

The Best of Ernie Pyle's World War II Dispatches. New York: Random House, 1986, p194.

3. Rommel, Erwin. *The Rommel Papers.* New York: Harcourt Brace & Co., 1953, p465.

4. Stalin, Joseph. *The Great Patriotic War of the Soviet Union.* New York: Greenwood Press, reprinted 1969, p86.

5. Guderian, Heinz. *Panzer Leader.* New York: Ballantine Books, 1957, p251-52.

6. Inver, Vera. *Leningrad Diary.* New York: St. Martin's Press, 1981, p39.

Chapter Six

1. Speer, Albert. *Inside the Third Reich.* New York. The Macmillan Company, New York: 1969, p366.

2. Liebling, A. J. *New Yorker Book of War Pieces.* New York: Schocken Books, compiled in 1947, p353.

3. *Life* magazine. March 19, 1945, p25.

4. Speer, Albert. *Inside the Third Reich.* New York: The Macmillan Company, 1969, p472-73.

Chapter Seven

1. Panter-Downes, Mollie. *New Yorker Book of War Pieces.* New York: Schocken Books, compiled in 1947, p473.

Further Reading

Blanco, Richard L. *The Luftwaffe in World War II.* New York: Messner, 1987.

Bliven, Bruce. *From Casablanca to Berlin: The War in North Africa and Europe.* New York: Random House, 1965.

Frank, Anne. *The Diary of a Young Girl.* New York: Doubleday, 1961.

Lawson, Don. *The French Resistance.* New York: Messner, 1984.

Markl, Julia. *The Battle of Britain.* New York: Watts, 1984.

Marrin, Albert. *Overlord: D-Day and the Invasion of Europe.* New York: Athenium, 1982.

Meltzer, Milton. *Never to Forget: The Jews of the Holocaust.* New York: Harper, 1976.

Ryan, Cornelius. *The Longest Day.* New York: Simon and Schuster, 1959.

Stein, R. Conrad. *The Road to Rome.* Chicago: Children's Press, 1984.

Stein, R. Conrad. *Hitler Youth.* Chicago: Children's Press, 1985.

Tulsa, Ann and Tulsa, John. *The Nuremberg Trial.* New York: Athenium, 1984.

Index

About the Author

R. Conrad Stein was born and raised in Chicago. He served in the U.S. Marine Corps in the mid-1950's, when the United States was at peace. After being discharged from the marines he attended the University of Illinois where he received a degree in history. Mr. Stein later earned an advanced degree from the University of Guanajuato in Mexico. The author lives in Chicago with his wife, Deborah Kent, who is also an author of books for young readers. They have a daughter, Janna.

The study of history is Mr. Stein's hobby. He thinks of the past as a special and very exciting world. Mr. Stein has written more than fifty history books for young readers.